THAT'S WHAT THEY SAID

Title: That's What They Said
Copyright © Red T Media, a division of Enable Training and Consulting Inc, 2023.

Finalist, Canadian Writer's Union Writing For Children Contest, 2006 (original version)

All rights reserved under International and Pan-American Copyright Conventions.
No part of this book may be reproduced or utilized in any form or by any means, electronically or mechanically, including scanning, photographing, photocopying, recording, or by any information storage and retrieval system without permission in writing from the publisher.

International Standard Book Number: 978-1-927425-34-3
Author: Amy Leask
Illustration and Design: Klaudia Maziec
Editor: Ben Zimmer

That's What They Said first edition published by:
Red T Kids' Media,
Milton, ON, Canada
www.RedTKidsMedia.com

For H.H., whose fabulous tall tales helped us learn to think.

They told me not to play with my belly button. They said if I did, my bum would fall off,

right in the middle of the floor,

and my pants would have nothing to hold them up anymore.

They told me if I kept on poking it, even after my bum fell off, my belly button would come unglued, and I'd spring a leak.

They said I'd fly around the room like a leaky balloon.

They told me if I played with my belly button, I'd wind up a huge, flat, wrinkly pile in the corner whose bum had fallen off and bounced away.

That's what they said.

They told me to always wash my ears.

They said that if I forgot, my ears would start to smell like cheese, and not the good kind of cheese either.

They said if I kept ignoring my ears, they'd not only smell like the worst stinky cheese…

...but that potatoes would start growing in them.

They told me if I didn't wash my ears, I'd become a walking,

talking

cheese factory and potato farm.

That's what they said.

They told me if I didn't eat the crusts on my sandwich, I wouldn't be able to see in the dark.

They told me if I didn't eat my crusts, I'd stub my toes on the way to the bathroom in the middle of the night.

They said if I couldn't see in the dark,

I'd get lost at Halloween,

and be wandering around the neighbourhood until winter came.

That's what they said.

They told me not to stick out my bottom lip when I got angry.

They said my bottom lip was just the right size for a bird to sit on.

They said that birds never travel alone, and pretty soon I'd have a whole flock of them, flapping and squawking and pecking at my freckles.

They said it would be just a matter of time before one of them decided to poop on my chin.

They said that birds never poop alone.

They said if I stuck out my bottom lip, I'd end up covered in noisy, pecky, poopy birds.

That's what they said.

They told me not to swallow my gum.

They warned me that gum stays in your body forever, or for at least

a million,

zillion

minutes.

They said it would have little parties with all the other gum I had swallowed, and soon, I'd be more gum than human, with no room in my stomach for anything else.

They said I'd have to miss Taco Tuesday… like,

ALL

Taco Tuesdays.

That's what they said.

But, luckily...

I didn't believe them.

I stuck my finger in my belly button, and my bum didn't try to escape.

    I listened as hard as I could, but I couldn't hear any leaks.

That night, I didn't wash my ears.

    There was no cheese, and definitely no potatoes in my ears.

I didn't eat the crusts on my sandwich.
>**I hid them in my socks.**
>>I made it to the bathroom just fine that night.

I stuck out my bottom lip as far as it would go.
>Not one bird came and pooped on me.

I still didn't swallow my gum, though,
>because,

>>well...

>**yech.**

I decided to give them some advice of my own.

I told them that all the tapping on their phones all the time would attract angry woodpeckers.

I told them wearing such

big,

thunky

shoes

would make them walk like Bigfoot,
and everyone would be scared and lock their doors,

and call in the scientists.

I told them that driving too fast would make the car tired, and it would melt like a big, goopy metal popsicle in the middle of the road.

I told them drinking too many of those

fancy,

floofy

coffees

would make it so that they never blinked again.

Finally, I told them that giving bad advice to little kids would make them look really, really silly.

That's what I said.